# Lacy Sunshine's Gnomes Coloring Book Pocket Edition Volume 23

I0455717

## Illustrated by Heather Valentin

©Heather Valentin. Lacy Sunshine. All rights reserved. No redistribution. No Pinning, No Sharing of these Line Art images without artist's Permission

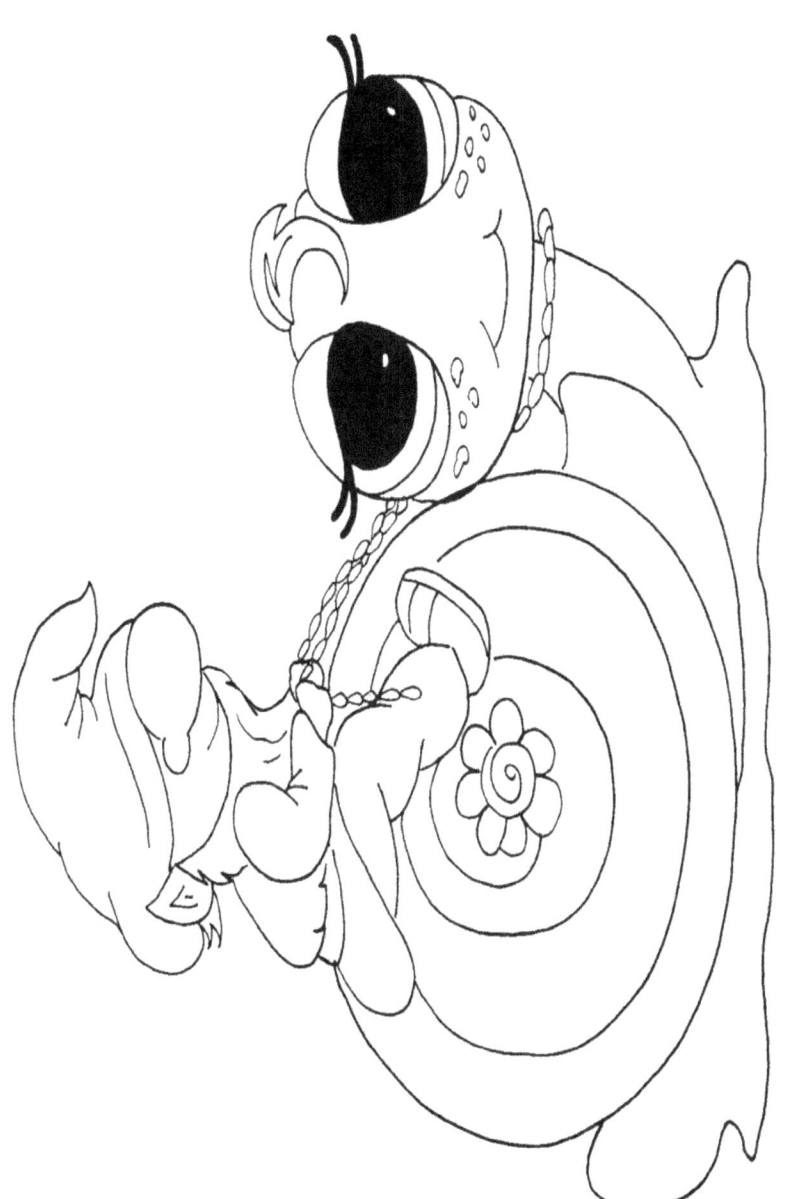

www.ingramcontent.com/pod-product-compliance
Lightning Source LLC
Chambersburg PA
CBHW060645290526
45793CB00001B/402